The Philosophy of Mark Twain

The Wit and Wisdom of a Literary Genius

DAVID GRAHAM

Copyright © 2014 David Graham

All rights reserved.

ISBN: 1502546019
ISBN-13: 978-1502546012

DISCLAIMER

Although every effort has been taken to ensure all information in this book is accurate, human error is always a possibility and therefore the author apologises in the event of any inaccuracies.

CONTENTS

Introduction	1
About Himself	3
About Mankind	7
General Philosophy	13
God & Religion	29
Humorous	35
Old Age & Death	43
Thoughts & Opinions	47

INTRODUCTION

Mark Twain (actually the pen name of Samuel Langhorne Clemens) was one of the best known and most unique authors of the 19th century. It is for very good reasons that his works have remained popular since his death in 1910.

Twain's best known works were undoubtedly *The Adventures of Tom Sawyer* and its sequel, *Adventures of Huckleberry Finn* (or 'The Great American Novel', as it is often referred to). He was renowned for the great wit and humour present in his works and conversation, deservedly earning him his reputation as the greatest humorist of his age. William Faulkner, in fact, called Twain 'the father of American literature'.

It is perhaps the timelessness of his humour that made Twain such a unique character of his time. Much of what he said and wrote appeals as much to the society of today as of his own era; some would argue even more so.

One subject Twain has been much quoted on is religion, though his true beliefs remain uncertain. He was known to be a Presbyterian, however was often critical of the nature and validity of organised religion.

Twain is perhaps one of the most quoted authors of his time, and certainly one of the most interesting. This book brings together some of the most amusing, interesting and thought-provoking comments from this literary genius.

ABOUT HIMSELF

"I must have a prodigious quantity of mind; it takes me as much as a week sometimes to make it up."

*

"My mother had a great deal of trouble with me, but I think she enjoyed it."

*

"I don't give a damn for a man that can only spell a word one way."

*

"I have been complimented many times and they always embarrass me; I always feel that they have not said enough."

*

"I can live for two months on a good compliment."

*

"My books are like water; those of the great geniuses are wine. (Fortunately) everybody drinks water."

*

"I have never taken any exercise, except sleeping and resting, and I never intend to take any."

*

"I was gratified to be able to answer promptly, and I did. I said I didn't know."

"When I was younger I could remember anything, whether it happened or not."

*

"I was seldom able to see an opportunity until it had ceased to be one."

*

"As an example to others, and not that I care for moderation myself, it has always been my rule never to smoke when asleep, and never to refrain from smoking when awake."

*

"I never smoke to excess - that is, I smoke in moderation, only one cigar at a time."

ABOUT MANKIND

"The man who is a pessimist before 48 knows too much; if he is an optimist after it, he knows too little."

*

"When a person cannot deceive himself the chances are against his being able to deceive other people."

*

"Everything human is pathetic. The secret source of humor itself is not joy but sorrow. There is no humor in heaven."

*

"A man cannot be comfortable without his own approval."

*

"A man who carries a cat by the tail learns something he can learn in no other way."

*

"It is just like man's vanity and impertinence to call an animal dumb because it is dumb to his dull perceptions."

*

"Humor is mankind's greatest blessing."

*

"Man is the only animal that blushes - or needs to."

*

"A round man cannot be expected to fit in a square hole right away. He must have time to modify his shape."

*

"Thousands of geniuses live and die undiscovered - either by themselves or by others."

*

"There are people who can do all fine and heroic things but one - keep from telling their happiness to the unhappy."

*

"There are times when one would like to hang the whole human race, and finish the farce."

*

"The human race has one really effective weapon, and

that is laughter."

*

"The human race is a race of cowards; and I am not only marching in that procession but carrying a banner."

*

"We are all alike, on the inside."

*

"A man is never more truthful than when he acknowledges himself a liar."

*

"Biographies are but the clothes and buttons of the man. The biography of the man himself cannot be written."

*

"Life would be infinitely happier if we could only be born at the age of eighty and gradually approach eighteen."

*

"Man will do many things to get himself loved, he will do all things to get himself envied."

*

"If man could be crossed with the cat it would improve man, but deteriorate the cat."

*

"What a wee little part of a person's life are his acts and his words! His real life is led in his head, and is known to none but himself."

*

"Laws control the lesser man... Right conduct controls the greater one."

DAVID GRAHAM

*

"It were not best that we should all think alike; it is difference of opinion that makes horse races."

*

"When people do not respect us we are sharply offended; yet in his private heart no man much respects himself."

GENERAL PHILOSOPHY

"Let us not be too particular; it is better to have old secondhand diamonds than none at all."

*

"A man's character may be learned from the adjectives which he habitually uses in conversation."

*

"Don't say the old lady screamed. Bring her on and let her scream."

*

"It is easier to stay out than get out."

*

"It is better to take what does not belong to you than to let it lie around neglected."

*

"Everything has its limit - iron ore cannot be educated into gold."

*

"When you fish for love, bait with your heart, not your brain."

*

"The best way to cheer yourself up is to try to cheer somebody else up."

*

"Prosperity is the best protector of principle."

*

"All emotion is involuntary when genuine."

*

"When in doubt tell the truth."

*

"Grief can take care if itself, but to get the full value of a joy you must have somebody to divide it with."

*

"Anger is an acid that can do more harm to the vessel in which it is stored than to anything on which it is poured."

*

"There are several good protections against temptation, but the surest is cowardice."

*

"Better a broken promise than none at all."

*

"The more things are forbidden, the more popular they become."

*

"Drag your thoughts away from your troubles... by the ears, by the heels, or any other way you can manage it."

*

"Don't part with your illusions. When they are gone, you may still exist, but you have ceased to live."

*

"Kindness is the language which the deaf can hear and the blind can see."

*

"Thunder is good, thunder is impressive; but it is lightning that does the work."

*

"To succeed in life, you need two things: ignorance and confidence."

*

"The wit knows that his place is at the tail of a procession."

*

"Noise proves nothing. Often a hen who has merely laid an egg cackles as if she laid an asteroid."

*

"It's not the size of the dog in the fight, it's the size of the fight in the dog."

*

"It ain't what you don't know that gets you into trouble. It's what you know for sure that just ain't so."

*

"Do the right thing. It will gratify some people and astonish the rest."

*

"If you tell the truth, you don't have to remember anything."

*

"Let us make a special effort to stop communicating with each other, so we can have some conversation."

*

"The lack of money is the root of all evil."

*

"The Public is merely a multiplied 'me.'"

*

"The trouble ain't that there is too many fools, but that the lightning ain't distributed right."

*

"Work consists of whatever a body is obliged to do. Play consists of whatever a body is not obliged to do."

*

"Loyalty to the country always. Loyalty to the government when it deserves it."

*

"When we remember we are all mad, the mysteries disappear and life stands explained."

*

"The rule is perfect: in all matters of opinion our adversaries are insane."

*

"You can't depend on your eyes when your imagination is out of focus."

*

"Loyalty to petrified opinion never yet broke a chain or freed a human soul."

*

"Principles have no real force except when one is well-fed."

*

"It is better to deserve honors and not have them than to have them and not deserve them."

*

"Courage is resistance to fear, mastery of fear, not absence of fear."

*

"Truth is stranger than fiction, but it is because Fiction is obliged to stick to possibilities; Truth isn't."

*

"Truth is mighty and will prevail. There is nothing wrong with this, except that it ain't so."

*

"Humor must not professedly teach and it must not

professedly preach, but it must do both if it would live forever."

*

"To be good is noble; but to show others how to be good is nobler and no trouble."

*

"Against the assault of laughter nothing can stand."

*

"Wrinkles should merely indicate where smiles have been."

*

"The right word may be effective, but no word was ever as effective as a rightly timed pause."

*

"It's no wonder that truth is stranger than fiction. Fiction has to make sense."

*

"Wit is the sudden marriage of ideas which, before their union, were not perceived to have any relation."

*

"Whenever you find yourself on the side of the majority, it is time to pause and reflect."

*

"Action speaks louder than words but not nearly as often."

*

"Work is a necessary evil to be avoided."

*

"Fiction is obliged to stick to possibilities. Truth isn't."

*

"Repartee is something we think of twenty-four hours too late."

*

"Forgiveness is the fragrance that the violet sheds on the heel that has crushed it."

*

"The secret of getting ahead is getting started."

*

"All you need is ignorance and confidence and the success is sure."

*

"Necessity is the mother of taking chances."

*

"Words are only painted fire; a look is the fire itself."

*

"A person with a new idea is a crank until the idea succeeds."

*

"It is curious that physical courage should be so common in the world and moral courage so rare."

*

"Don't go around saying the world owes you a living. The world owes you nothing. It was here first."

*

"Few things are harder to put up with than the

annoyance of a good example."

*

"Do the thing you fear most and the death of fear is certain."

*

"Nothing so needs reforming as other people's habits."

*

"There is a charm about the forbidden that makes it unspeakably desirable."

*

"Civilization is the limitless multiplication of unnecessary necessities."

*

"Good breeding consists in concealing how much we think of ourselves and how little we think of the other person."

*

"Be careless in your dress if you must, but keep a tidy soul."

GOD & RELIGION

"It ain't those parts of the Bible that I can't understand that bother me, it is the parts that I do understand."

*

"Often it does seem such a pity that Noah and his party did not miss the boat."

*

"Man was made at the end of the week's work, when God was tired."

*

"Under certain circumstances, urgent circumstances, desperate circumstances, profanity provides a relief denied even to prayer."

*

"If Christ were here now there is one thing he would not be—a Christian."

*

"All right, then, I'll go to hell."

*

"It is by the goodness of God that in our country we have those three unspeakably precious things: freedom of speech, freedom of conscience, and the prudence never to practice either of them."

*

"Faith is believing what you know ain't so."

*

"God made the Idiot for practice, and then He made the School Board."

*

"No sinner is ever saved after the first twenty minutes of a sermon."

*

"In the first place, God made idiots. That was for practice. Then he made school boards."

*

"The Christian's Bible is a drug store. Its contents remain the same, but the medical practice changes."

*

"Martyrdom covers a multitude of sins."

*

"Only one thing is impossible for God: To find any sense in any copyright law on the planet."

*

"But who prays for Satan? Who, in eighteen centuries, has had the common humanity to pray for the one sinner that needed it most?"

*

"Prophesy is a good line of business, but it is full of risks."

*

"Go to Heaven for the climate, Hell for the company."

*

"I don't like to commit myself about heaven and hell - you see, I have friends in both places."

HUMOROUS

"Denial ain't just a river in Egypt."

*

"Name the greatest of all inventors. Accident."

*

"Get your facts first, then you can distort them as you please."

*

"It usually takes me more than three weeks to prepare a good impromptu speech."

*

"Cauliflower is nothing but cabbage with a college education."

*

"Giving up smoking is the easiest thing in the world. I know because I've done it thousands of times."

*

"She was not quite what you would call refined. She was not quite what you would call unrefined. She was the kind of person that keeps a parrot."

*

"What is the difference between a taxidermist and a tax collector? The taxidermist takes only your skin."

*

"What, sir, would the people of the earth be without woman? They would be scarce, sir, almighty scarce."

*

"Never put off till tomorrow what you can do the day after tomorrow."

*

"Suppose you were an idiot, and suppose you were a member of Congress; but I repeat myself."

*

"Soap and education are not as sudden as a massacre, but they are more deadly in the long run."

*

"We have the best government that money can buy."

*

"When angry, count to four; when very angry, swear."

*

"He is now rising from affluence to poverty."

*

"The first of April is the day we remember what we are the other 364 days of the year."

*

"Only kings, presidents, editors, and people with tapeworms have the right to use the editorial 'we.'"

*

"Buy land, they're not making it anymore."

*

"It is better to keep your mouth closed and let people think you are a fool than to open it and remove all doubt."

*

"When red-haired people are above a certain social grade their hair is auburn."

*

"Honesty is the best policy - when there is money in it."

*

"Familiarity breeds contempt - and children."

*

"If it's your job to eat a frog, it's best to do it first thing in the morning. And If it's your job to eat two frogs, it's best to eat the biggest one first."

*

"To refuse awards is another way of accepting them with more noise than is normal."

*

"If the world comes to an end, I want to be in Cincinnati. Everything comes there ten years later."

*

"It's good sportsmanship to not pick up lost golf balls while they are still rolling."

*

"Do not tell fish stories where the people know you; but particularly, don't tell them where they know the fish."

*

"'Classic.' A book which people praise and don't read."

*

"All generalizations are false, including this one."

*

"Golf is a good walk spoiled."

*

"By trying we can easily learn to endure adversity. Another man's, I mean."

*

"How lucky Adam was. He knew when he said a good thing, nobody had said it before."

*

"It was wonderful to find America, but it would have been more wonderful to miss it."

OLD AGE & DEATH

"Why is it that we rejoice at a birth and grieve at a funeral? It is because we are not the person involved."

*

"I didn't attend the funeral, but I sent a nice letter saying I approved of it."

*

"Lord save us all from old age and broken health and a hope tree that has lost the faculty of putting out blossoms."

*

"The fear of death follows from the fear of life. A man who lives fully is prepared to die at any time."

*

"Age is an issue of mind over matter. If you don't mind, it doesn't matter."

*

"Be careful about reading health books. You may die of a misprint."

*

"When your friends begin to flatter you on how young you look, it's a sure sign you're getting old."

*

"The reports of my death have been greatly exaggerated."

*

"I am an old man and have known a great many troubles, but most of them never happened."

*

"Let us endeavor so to live so that when we come to die even the undertaker will be sorry."

THOUGHTS & OPINIONS

"There is no distinctly American criminal class - except Congress."

*

"Education consists mainly of what we have unlearned."

*

"Ideally a book would have no order to it, and the reader would have to discover his own."

*

"George Washington, as a boy, was ignorant of the commonest accomplishments of youth. He could not even lie."

*

"The public is the only critic whose opinion is worth anything at all."

*

"Substitute 'damn' every time you're inclined to write 'very'; your editor will delete it and the writing will be just as it should be."

*

"In the Spring, I have counted 136 different kinds of weather inside of 24 hours."

*

"The finest clothing made is a person's own skin, but, of course, society demands something more than this."

*

"The only way to keep your health is to eat what you don't want, drink what you don't like, and do what you'd rather not."

*

"Facts are stubborn, but statistics are more pliable."

*

"Never pick a fight with people who buy ink by the barrel."

*

"Water, taken in moderation, cannot hurt anybody."

*

"There are basically two types of people. People who

accomplish things, and people who claim to have accomplished things. The first group is less crowded."

*

"The educated Southerner has no use for an 'r', except at the beginning of a word."

*

"The very ink with which history is written is merely fluid prejudice."

*

"The main difference between a cat and a lie is that a cat only has nine lives."

*

"There are lies, damned lies and statistics."

*

"The difference between the almost right word and the right word is really a large matter - 'tis the difference between the lightning-bug and the lightning."

*

"Truth is the most valuable thing we have. Let us economize it."

*

"Patriot: the person who can holler the loudest without knowing what he is hollering about."

*

"We Americans... bear the ark of liberties of the world."

*

"The more you explain it, the more I don't understand it."

*

"Many a small thing has been made large by the right kind of advertising."

*

"Climate is what we expect, weather is what we get."

*

"I've never let my school interfere with my education."

*

"Apparently there is nothing that cannot happen today."

*

"There is no sadder sight than a young pessimist."

*

"Part of the secret of a success in life is to eat what you like and let the food fight it out inside."

*

"A person who won't read has no advantage over one who can't read."

*

"Good friends, good books and a sleepy conscience: this is the ideal life."

*

"Sometimes too much to drink is barely enough."

*

"The most interesting information comes from children, for they tell all they know and then stop."

*

"Clothes make the man. Naked people have little or no influence on society."

ALSO BY DAVID GRAHAM

Inside the Mind of George Bernard Shaw

The Very Best of Ralph Waldo Emerson

The Very Best of Clint Eastwood

The Very Best of Roger Moore

The Very Best of Kirk Douglas

The Very Best of Friedrich Nietzsche

Printed in Great Britain
by Amazon